Whose Sound Is This?

Whose Is It?
Science

A Look at Animal Noises—
Chirps, Clicks, and Hoots

Written by Nancy Kelly Allen

Illustrated by Derrick Alderman
and Denise Shea

PICTURE WINDOW BOOKS
Minneapolis, Minnesota

Special thanks to our advisers for their expertise:

Debbie Folkerts, Ph.D.
Assistant Professor of Biological Sciences
Auburn University, Alabama

Susan Kesselring, M.A., Literacy Educator
Rosemount-Apple Valley-Eagan (Minnesota) School District

Managing Editors: Bob Temple, Catherine Neitge
Creative Director: Terri Foley
Editors: Nadia Higgins, Patricia Stockland
Editorial Adviser: Andrea Cascardi
Storyboard Development: Amy Bailey Muehlenhardt
Designer: Nathan Gassman
Page production: Banta
The illustrations in this book were prepared digitally.

Picture Window Books
5115 Excelsior Boulevard
Suite 232
Minneapolis, MN 55416
877-845-8392
www.picturewindowbooks.com

Printed in the United States of America.

Library of Congress Cataloging-in-Publication Data
Allen, Nancy Kelly, 1949-
Whose sound is this? : a look at animal noises—chirps,
clicks, and hoots / by Nancy Kelly Allen ; illustrated by
Derrick Alderman and Denise Shea.
p. cm. — (Whose is it?)
Includes bibliographical references (p.   ).
ISBN 1-4048-0610-5 (reinforced library binding)
1. Animal sounds—Juvenile literature. I. Alderman, Derrick,
ill. II. Shea, Denise, ill. III. Title. IV. Series.

QL765.A46 2004
591.59'4—dc22
2004000880

Shhh. Let's listen to find who's who.

Start noticing the sounds of animals. An animal sound can be a quick chirp or a long rattle. It can be a soft moan or a mighty roar. It can be a *click click click* or a *hee-haw, hee-haw.*

Some sounds mean keep out! Others say come closer. Some sounds help animals keep track of one another. Other sounds help them find their way in the dark.

Animal noises don't all sound alike because they don't all work alike.

Can you tell whose sound is whose?

Look in the back for more fun facts about animal sounds.

Whose sound is this, with the **A R R R**

4

RRRRR?

This is a lion's roar.

A lion cub has wandered too far from its mother. *Arrrr!* The mother calls her baby back. Adult lions also roar to let one another know where they are.

Fun fact: Big cats, such as lions, tigers, jaguars, and leopards, can roar but not purr. All other cats can purr but not roar.

Whose sound is this, with the CLICK CLICK CLICK?

This is a dolphin's sound.

A bottlenose dolphin's clicking sounds make echoes. They bounce off objects such as boats and fish. The dolphin listens for these echoes. The echoes help the animal find its way through the dark ocean.

Fun fact: Each dolphin makes its own special whistling sound. None of their voices sound exactly alike.

Whose sound is this, with the WHOOOOO

WHOO WHOO WHOOOOO?

This is an owl's sound.

As night falls, a great horned owl starts to hoot. The male's loud, low call tells other males to stay out of his territory. *Whooooo whoo whoo whooooo* means, "Find your own roost!"

Fun fact: Great horned owls often *whoo whoo* back when people *whoo whoo* to them.

Whose sound is this, with the JUG-O-RUM, JUG-O-RUM?

This is a bullfrog's sound.

A male bullfrog hops into a pond on a warm spring night. *Jug-o-rum, jug-o-rum.* His low grumbling call makes a female choose him as her mate. In a few weeks, little wriggling tadpoles will hatch in the pond.

Fun fact: Some kinds of frogs have bags of skin under their chins. When they croak, the bags fill up like balloons. The frogs' calls grow even louder.

Whose sound is this,

with the HEE-HAW,

HEE-HAW?

13

This is a donkey's bray.

This donkey is upset! A donkey likes to be fed at the same time every day. If the meal is late, the donkey will *hee-haw* until someone brings dinner.

Fun fact: Donkeys are mostly quiet animals. They usually only bray when they want to complain.

Whose sound is this,

with the CHIRP CHIRP CHIRP?

15

This is a grasshopper's sound.

A male grasshopper rubs his back legs against his front wings. His body works like a violin and bow. The grasshopper plays *chirp chirp chirp* to get noticed by a female.

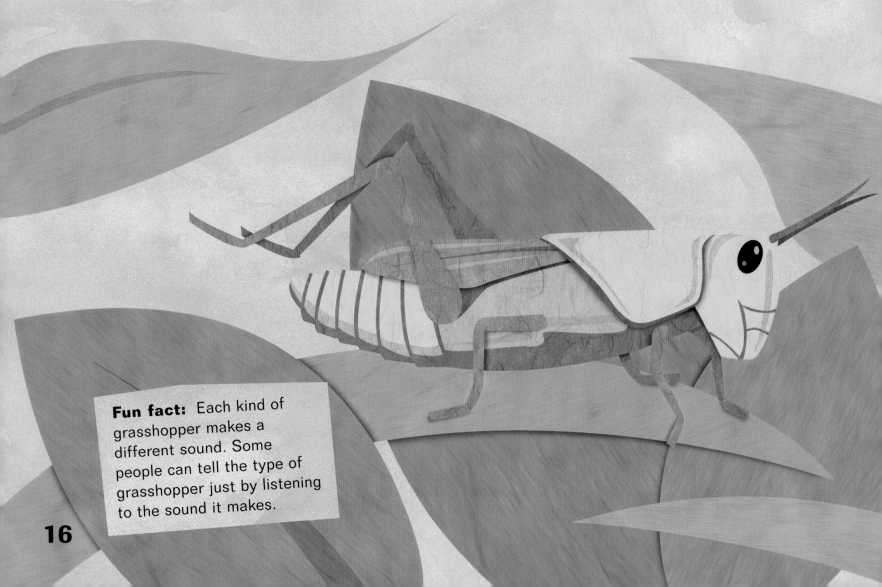

Fun fact: Each kind of grasshopper makes a different sound. Some people can tell the type of grasshopper just by listening to the sound it makes.

Whose sound is this, with the **Ch Ch Ch Ch Ch Ch Ch Ch Ch ?**

17

This is a rattlesnake's sound.

Watch out! When a rattlesnake shakes its rattle, it is reminding people and animals that it can deliver a painful bite. The snake can shake its rattle up to 50 times a second to make a long *ch-ch-ch-ch-ch-ch*.

Fun fact: A baby rattlesnake doesn't have a rattle. As the snake grows, it will shed its skin many times. Parts of these old skins are what form the sections of the rattle.

Whose sound is this, with the WHOOOO-HOOOO, GO, GO, GO?

That's you, cheering for your team!

That's just one of the many sounds you make. You also sing. You laugh and cry. You yell and whisper. You clap your hands and stomp your feet. What other sounds can you make?

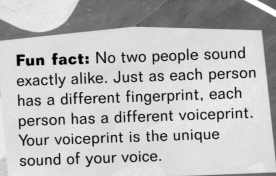

Fun fact: No two people sound exactly alike. Just as each person has a different fingerprint, each person has a different voiceprint. Your voiceprint is the unique sound of your voice.

20

Just for Fun

Animal Sounds Around the World

A dog says "woof," and a pig says "oink," right? Not necessarily. Woof and oink are how we say those animal sounds in English. Other languages have their own words for animal noises. Try saying some of these:

	Dog	Duck	Pig
English	*woof; ruff*	*quack quack*	*oink oink*
Chinese	*wang wang*	*gua gua*	*hu-lu hu-lu*
Japanese	*wanwan*	*gaa gaa*	*buubuu*
Russian	*gaf-gaf*	*krya-krya*	*khryu-khryu*

Fun Facts About Animal Sounds

Gobble Gobble ... Click Click

A male turkey gobbles when he hears loud noises or when he is looking for a mate. He gobbles when he settles in to sleep at night. A female turkey makes a clicking sound.

What's So Funny?

A hyena is a noisy animal that often sounds like a person giggling. It makes a giggling sound when it catches a meal or senses danger. When a hyena greets another hyena, it squeals softly.

Better Watch What You Say!

A parrot can say real words. Some parrots can tell jokes and make speeches. A parrot doesn't really understand what it is saying. It is just repeating the sounds it hears.

Noisy Beach

A sea lion can make many different sounds. It can click, whistle, and make a noise that sounds like a ringing bell. A male sea lion barks like a dog to defend its home. Females call to their pups. Each mother's call is unique. A pup can pick out the special sound of its mother among thousands of other sea lions lying together on a beach.

Underwater Rhythm

A male red drum fish makes noises that sound like a beating drum. His underwater song gets a female red drum fish to notice him.

Coo Coo on the Run

The roadrunner is a kind of cuckoo. Before making a call, the bird lowers its wings and lifts its tail. A coo coo soon follows. A roadrunner coos when it is frightened or curious. It will also call out to find another roadrunner.

Useful Trumpet

An elephant raises its trunk in the air and blows. It makes a loud noise that sounds like a trumpet's call. That call warns other elephants of danger. Elephants also make trumpet sounds when they fight.

Words to Know

hatch—to break out of an egg

mates—a male animal and a female animal that come together to make baby animals

shed—when old skin comes off and new, roomier skin is uncovered

tadpole—a baby frog that swims in water and looks like a fish

territory—the special area in which an animal lives; an animal doesn't like it when some outsiders come into its territory

voiceprint—the special patterns of a person's voice

To Learn More

At the Library

George, Jean Craighead. *How to Talk to Your Cat.* New York: HarperCollins, 2000.

Kaner, Etta. *Animal Talk: How Animals Communicate Through Sight, Sound, and Smell.* Toronto: Kids Can Press, 2002.

McDaniel, Melissa. *Animal Talk.* Tarrytown, N.Y.: Benchmark Books, 2002.

Pfeffer, Wendy. *Sounds All Around.* New York: HarperCollins, 1999.

On the Web

FactHound offers a safe, fun way to find Web sites related to this book. All of the sites on FactHound have been researched by our staff. *www.facthound.com*

1. Visit the FactHound home page.
2. Enter a search word related to this book, or type in this special code: 1404806105.
3. Click the FETCH IT button.

Your trusty FactHound will fetch the best Web sites for you!

Index

Look for all the books in this series:

Whose Ears Are These?
A Look at Animal Ears—Short,
Flat, and Floppy

Whose Eyes Are These?
A Look at Animal Eyes—Big,
Round, and Narrow

Whose Feet Are These?
A Look at Hooves, Paws, and Claws

Whose Food Is This?
A Look at What Animals Eat—
Leaves, Bugs, and Nuts

Whose House Is This?
A Look at Animal Homes—Webs,
Nests, and Shells

Whose Legs Are These?
A Look at Animal Legs—Kicking,
Running, and Hopping

Whose Mouth Is This?
A Look at Bills, Suckers, and Tubes

Whose Nose Is This?
A Look at Beaks, Snouts, and Trunks

Whose Shadow Is This?
A Look at Animal Shapes—Round,
Long, and Pointy

Whose Skin Is This?
A Look at Animal Skin—Scaly,
Furry, and Prickly

Whose Sound Is This?
A Look at Animal Noises—Chirps,
Clicks, and Hoots

Whose Spots Are These?
A Look at Animal Markings—Round,
Bright, and Big

Whose Tail Is This?
A Look at Tails—Swishing,
Wiggling, and Rattling

Whose Work Is This?
A Look at the Things Animals
Make—Pearls, Milk, and Honey